*To my parents, who've supported me every step
of the way.*

*To Sru, Gamyum and Rav who have always
been my greatest muses.*

ACKNOWLEDGEMENT

Thank you to all the people who've lived inside of me and given me their stories.

PREFACE

Surrealism is my preferred reality
I don't want to be defined or asked to define
myself. It's such a weird thing to be one thing.
people say that people don't change so how do I
explain that I'm changing every single day
I've been existing this way and wish to whoosh
over people's heads as this fluid creature, of
variable nature, something that changes its
shape, with different appendages and limbs and
adornments and embellishments every single
time your eyes manage to catch a glimpse of it.
In my mind's eye i have nine arms and so many
wings and eyes all over
Tongues hidden in orifices in places you'd never
expect them to be, each fluent in a different
language.
I wish to be this translucent, paradoxically
iridescent beast whose textures and organs
systems reflect the environment around it, not
just merely correspond but adapt to conquer.
I don't want to be an actual person, that seems
counterintuitive to the ingenious and insane
nature of the human mind.

The Tenebrous Timepiece

A black timepiece sits on my desk, it's golden
hands and golden fingers tingle at my behest,
It's face is contorted, the closest thing to a frown,
It sneers at me, and growls at my gown,
That I will never don again
Nor will I ever put on my crown,
So cleverly crafted from hands folded and
sinews of a disheartened clown,
That I happened to have flogged every now and
then.
The time doesn't tick away, it simply stands still,
A screaming reminder of a gentleman's
goodwill,
Towards me as I flutter and float over the hearts
of most,
They sigh and shudder at my disposition and
then a shrill
Cry as they see the mascara run and the makeup
dry, it was time for me to kill,
They who opposed what I would've then boast,
About a watch with no legs that talks to Me and
calls me deary,
Tells me tales of misfortune and often makes me
weary

Of the life I have led and the hardships yet to
come,
But I don't let it get down, but simply dirty,
Willing to do things other consider horribly
eerie,
And dreadful and dangerous but I do them for
they make me numb
Numb to pain and sadness and happiness all the
same
Throw away the geese, the gander and all the
fame,
Festering and harmful, thrown out onto the
chopping block,
They did not know I was a master at their game
They thought they had me cornered, thought
they would extinguish my flame,
For they knew not of my trusty advisor my black
tempest, my wily little clock.
Now it lies at my bedside even a thousand years
after we met
It's face covered in grime and dust, and still it
does fret
For others have emerged from the depths of my
labyrinth of a mind,
No longer ostentatious it slowly tries to beget
The same feeling of being drowned and
hopelessly trapped but I cannot let,
It shroud my ears with deception and whispers
of death or stifle my cold breath

For I cannot see the map, cannot see the land,
the others had already made me blind.

Absconsion

Aftermath of accolades,
Lost boy: torn gutter his only home is the Ace of
Spades,
A chicken coop nestled between the hills,
Betwixt the rain and the cheap thrills,
Mold on the bottom of his feet,
Scars on his back from when he managed to
retreat,
From that festering core of heartless reprieve,
T'was a maimed hut, that crippled hotel,
An abandoned amusement
A gory citadel of deities still worshipped,
Not dark gods but fairies and wishes
Granted without a thought or price to be paid,
Of the dirty excise that they'd have to trade
For some spice in their life: a misplaced crusade
And so the boy bolted towards that happy
serenade
Of loving families and cool Lemonade
Bathing in the sunlight, But his Eyes forbade
Him to look up, at the sweltering cascade of
water and salt,
Drudgery through the years, beaten at the whim
of a single malt,
Growing into a young man, it wasn't his fault,

But his skin grew thicker to withstand their
assault,
So much of unsanctioned decay he simply
abhorred,
An un-Responsibility he never asked for,
He hurriedly scampered through the
shortcomings of his mother,
Stumbled across the long list of vices he owed to
his father,
Then then tripped over
And into the grave of his abuse: still celebrated
The only reason he would call himself
dilapidated,
A cherished memory of his humanity being
castrated,
A monster raised by savages,
His past seemed to have been antiquated
So very long ago
Could he perhaps try to evade it?
Or would he still want to be evicted?
From this husk of a man he called
Myself
Panting,
he now reached a carousel on the sea shore
Looked down at himself
Too old now to go on the rides,
Too young to cause any kind of uproar
Life fell apart, he just stopped keeping score
Cursed at the middle, telltale of a sophomore

Only place left to go
Was the mythical candy store,
Slipping in as a little boy again, his tongue
ached of sugar and bitter detriment,
Back to a time before he met his best friend
Resentment,
When sentiment wasn't an impediment,
And merriment always seemed imminent,
Now nothing yet persists but sediments of
coloured glass
Lost in a spectrum of his final testament
And Will.

Puzzle Pieces

Oh lover of mine
Collapsingstars puke polka dots periodically
If I could catch them all and stitch them onto a
dress made of moonshine I'd keel over and turn
to spaghetti in space
Someday you will die
I'd prefer it were by my hand but I won't
complain if you happen to explode into seven
million different colours spontaneously
I'll be lurking within the embroidery of your
lingerie as you disintegrate
Following you into the dark with the taste of
December still fresh on my lips
And by that I just mean the salt from the snot
that dribbled down as I was dozing,
There are no tunnels or gates to easy nightmares
but white hot fever dreams we have to moan
through to try and escape
We have our hands clasped tight through the
night as we try to fit our hips together like
puzzle pieces while heaven and hell try to decide
where to grant us release, to see if they'll be
satisfied by the taste we left on each other's
necks,

Do we wait for the humming buzz of the neon
exit signs telling us that they lack all vacancies
or do we skedaddle at the break of- day?
How does time pass in a place between places,
Madame, would you do me the honor of
tumbling through the void
Would it hurt if there's no one beside you as
your soul embarks into some twisted metal
version of your school,
Turtles with Razer sharp teeth and oak trees with
crude silver wings
Where a woman cloaked in honeysuckle fireflies
from head to toe with somber shuttered eyes that
burn like frozen winter nights beats your
knuckles like you've never known before,
Where your best friend has a tongue of shadows
and there's a crocodile for a substitute teacher
behind every door,
There's a song playing through the corridors that
says fear is love, that fear is what brings you
home by dawn
You and me, we could see everything from
Tokyo to Calgary, wearing down the soles of our
shoes.

Remember, the beginning and the end

I think about my friends a lot
Their lives, their failures, their loves, whether
they know they're saviors
They don't know where I am
Sending hearts emojis when I pop up in a game
of whack a mole in another city
Telling me they like the guacamole I made from
rotting avocados plucked from the wrong tree
I miss their stories
The stuff they leave behind in my room and my
memories
The good they leave in their wake
Never ripples but gentle waves
And the destruction they create
But beyond it all
I remember the love
I find it hard to make them know how much I
love them, I'm too selfish
I order food to scarf down by myself and
halfway through wonder how it'd be so much
better if all our mouths could taste the same
things
I remember sitting on my grandfather's knee as
he kissed my cheek with his deadly moustache,

while he drunkenly told me about the man he
killed in his clinic by giving him the wrong kind
of medicine
I remember the girl with three braids asking me
if she could play with my diplodocus and
kicking me in the shins when I corrected her and
said it was a brachiosaurus
I remember falling off a staircase in my
grandmother's garden
While cousins who's names I don't remember
who I've never met again picked wings off of
ladybugs
Even though that probably didn't happen
Because she died before I was born
There were so many mangoes there then
A lot of anger, but a lot of mangoes too
I've forgotten the color of where i come from
Now my taste is me and
Of late it's been bitter
The sky is dead outside
It makes me think this world is easy to leave
behind
It's important to remember that the body leaves
the soul and not the other way around
I feel like someone else's dream sometimes
Until i remember the smell of my skin and
realise no one else would bother taking the time
She aimed right between my eyes

A bullet full of love ricocheting off of her
insidious affirmation and lies
But she forgot that the heart is where all the
action is
Shoutout to all the ghosts who've lived under my
bed
I love you

Waking up, a beginning and end

I've never woken up naked and in peace
An itch or a screech always precedes paranoia
regarding where I went to sleep
I used to eat my reflection and feel full
So full
Eager for more to gleam
Now I pace up and down the street outside my
house searching for people to beat
Turn to pulp with my feet, press into paper and
write poetry about my recurring quiet retreats
into my self
I love myself too much maybe
Being inside me makes me forget all the harsh
ineptitudes of facing reality
Does it really seem like I care about what's
happening to me?
Crab trotting across a road narrowly avoiding
passing cars as I spin and sweep
my coat tails across dead leaves
I wish I could witness my demons' dreams
When I last saw nishita
She hugged me without reprieve
In her silent sighs she told me she never wanted
to see or speak to me ever again in my life

All those calls I made to her landline in the
middle of the night probably made her parents
want to rip my skin from my body
She didn't get it
Nobody does
I can't remember the last time I woke up without
an alarm, probably would sleep forever if left
alone
If you stand on your head and really ponder
Life should never really be without wonder
If I could just figure out why that old man with
the pale orange crocodile skin shoes clapped as
he was walking behind me
I'd feel so much better
At ease
What war did he fight in
What wars have I been fighting
It's not normal to sit outside a friend's apartment
scared to go in while watching anime music
videos high as a kite
What even is normal
Don't forget all the tangents leading out of
introspective wormholes
Do you think I'm normal?
Please don't say you think I'm normal
Please for fucks sake
I'm not a black hole
Tell me I'm weird and I'll feel better in the
morning

I don't know what you want from me
I'm not good at figuring out how I need to alter
my personality
To stop hurting the people I love
Something to contemplate
Someone told me once that if you sneeze six
times in a row you can feel your brain start to
drop down your nose
I just sneezed nine times
But I'm not interested in finding out
I'm just tired
So tired
Things didn't happen the way i wanted them to
Something went wrong
Something went really wrong a while back
And i don't know
One morning you'll wake up and want to shave
your head
Because the snow that's falling from up there
won't stop until you're in a blizzard
Where everything burns in white flames
I was crazy once
But now I just want to live
There's so much in the world it makes me cry
There's good bad mad sad ugly happy
But I'm just obsessed with beauty
And it breaks my brain

Splurg Splurg

I'm raw silk spilling out of a cocoon
I'm milk dripping from the tit of a baboon
I am the broken mirrors on the floor of a
flooding bathroom
I am the cuts on my body that aren't going away
no matter what i do
No matter how many times i touch them with
my blade or my perfume
They sting and they cry and they won't let me
die
And petals blossom where scabs should grow
Death kisses me and tells me it's time to go
My bones are stubborn, hardened lazy even
Not ready to sink into the soil where they came
from
Wait, they need more calcium
Death why don't you sit down and crack open a
cold one, I'm not ready to die but you look like
you've been on your lonesome for too long and
that's just horribly wrong you've been escorting
all these sappy souls, and then there's me with
all these holes like on a beach you fit your feet
and the water from my cheeks rush in and fill
them with muck and ghosts and excuses to why I

haven't grown, now now why am I doing all the
talking
I said I'd listen and I've left you here gawking
surely you've seen worse, children expunged and
planets bursting, species choking and people
roasting all around you while you dance,
Two stepping to the sound of a knife ripping into
intestines, Tut Tut splurg splurg
You're so good you should take it up
professionally, people take you for granted
When you really think about it

Kintsugi

We tore through the weekend
Had a lazy Sunday
So dazed we skipped our meals
Plagued by the possibility of a dinner date gone
wrong and bad dreams
We got no sleep
Our bodies buzzing

I had a fever
My forehead burning
Until my hips joined yours under
Sheets you hog till my feet slip out
Drape yourself in the heat from my back
You make me cool
Until my face flushes red then grey and splits
into pixels of confusion
When i do something stupid

I always say I'll be alright
People tell me it is what it is and shove their
feelings under the carpet or be quiet until my
hands move
I just thought I'd be able to hold myself together
Without having to need people forever

Love bandaged across holes that keep getting
bigger
How much of what they give do I keep pouring
in
Like a bowl slowly losing water
Filling my cracks with gold
What's the point of being beautiful without
getting better

I'm fine now, can't stop the laughter
Couldn't breathe so i took off my dainty sweater
Walking at 3am in the dead of winter
You become one with all the things don't matter
That sigh and shake their heads, whipping up a
wind that only gets colder

Look I didn't want to be this kind of guy
Im crying outside your house with strangers
Shoot me with tranquilizers and tell them I'll be
alright
Drag me inside and let me spend the night
You can throw on glitter and do what you want
to my face
Run your hands over my body and braid my hair
Just throw me in the dumpster at first light
I want to be macerated
Stick a note on my forehead
When I'm in my spaceship I'll come to think of
you

While I'm sitting with my legs out of the airlock
Tunnel visioned with an impossible view

Mon vilain

Spring was never waiting for us
It ran one step ahead, out of the door in a hurry
tripping on the threshold and bleeding from the
nose after sneezing a hundred times
We followed in her dance between the parted
pages and untethered romances, Pressed in love's
hot fevered iron like a striped fox's snout
sniffing for fresh crimes

Sometimes as I sit melting in the dark
Sweet green icing flowing down my cheeks,
I watch your sleeping face, lit in the glow of a
flickering tv, the last thirty minutes of a movie
you've never seen providing the soundtrack to
your dreams,
I get distracted by the purple shadows creeping
up from under your feet, your perfect calves
caress my knuckles as i slot my hands into the
pits behind your knees,
Failing to hear the downpour beating down on
the street, I realise my cats have left my
brownies out in the rain, should've eaten more
to forget about the pain, start pulling out my hair
cos I can't take it, cos it took so long to bake it,

and i might never get that recipe from your brain
again

I recall often, your yellow cotton dress, the frills
you love to have bouncing bout your shoulders
always tickling my ears when I lay my head to
rest, imagining the hem of your skirt,
Foaming like a soft wave,
On the ground up till about your knees,
And my hands with a sharpie drawing birds and
bees on your thighs before you get tickly and
twist my wrist to unnatural degrees in your
tickle drunken stupor where you fail to believe
my pleas for release and plans to squeeze fingers
thinking I'll strike again while you're wheezing,
when you know I'm just teasing, so you start to
relax and embrace until you feel a warm breeze
on your neck and the titillation consumes your
intentions to be free from little hairs on my face
and subtract the space between your body and
mine till you feel the bass from within my chest
and breathe deeply,
A warmth begins to spread through your breast,
who'd have guessed that this idiot would have
passed your tests, a jester who used to keep you
perpetually stressed now gets you undressed as a
part of the main quest and now he's obsessed
with the folds in your skin and the arch of your
back and he wipes your chin after he bites your

lips instead of grabbing a snack, you did admit
he has a knack for being devastatingly
disarming, you grin as you smack his ass and I
know I've been bad but i made you a promise
and I intend to keep it
There could be another song for me but i wont
sing it
There could be another dream for me but I don't
need it
I will drink my wine while it is warm
And hold you until Ra decides to let loose a
solar storm and wipe out all life in the boldest
performance he's ever had to put on,
And after all the loves of my life,
I think of you and wonder why or what's
different this time and realise that it's not the
gifts or the rhymes but that it's pure and not
applied physics, not coincidence that keeps us
together,
But the love and wonder that we hold for each
other
I will take my life into my hands and use it
I will win the worship of every eye on the planet
and probably lose it
I will have all the things i desire
Let my mind grow and control the rivers of the
sky, have my fingers set on fire, do evil and only
get higher, ride the wind when I choose it, and
be the best liar

Oh but it might all be for naught if my fish
sandwich turns into a ghost and doesn't stay mon
vilain, by my side, my liaison to a world that's
better than the one we're currently reside in,
conclusions foregone and undecided if she
doesn't command protons or save the Amazon
while adorning the finest chiffon, upper echelon,
I might be turning nine thousand seven hundred
and eighty four but your twenty one far outranks
me and then some.

Colliding stars/Cry on my shoulder

I stab myself with a five fingered fork
Hoping all five senses come to a stop focusing
on the sensation of cold metal squirming it's way
through my epidermal eccentricities
I want to know you by your skin,
I'd like to think I know you better than anyone
else but I'm scared it doesn't mean much because
you're an enigma beyond anyone's
comprehension,
Glimpsing a sliver of divinity doesn't help you
understand its intricate complexities, but that's
another excuse on my behalf for not being able
to voice the extremities of you,
Now I'm broke and on my ass and it seems like
the start of so many stories of great people
who've bounced back but I'm stuck to the bottom
of our bed, hoping you'll come back to cut me
out of the iceberg ready to sink my life's ship,
I'm sorry for not being revolutionary enough to
commandeer life's rebelling assholes, I'm sorry
for being weak that way, the mast of my ship
swaying like a willow tree bent at the most
obtuse of angles unaware to anyone except your
acute observations, mostly because I convince

everyone and everything including myself that
the storm is the best way to proceed and through
it all
We've slipped away
We've found a place for us two to hide
And I'm happy in this rabbit hole just you and I
Colliding stars shiver in the heat of our throes, I
gasp for breath when I turn my head up and out
of my woes, counting till five as I suck on your
pretty marbled toes, whatever you say in your
petty sadistic misdemeanor is what goes, I only
put words in my mouth after I'm sure that they
do the most damage or in other words without
thinking at all, I drive you up the wall and I
bathe in your tears yearning to kiss you, jumping
up like a child as if your hair were mistletoe
But I know it'll be alright, I'll write the music
and stay up all night trying to sing and make
things bright, I'll put you to sleep with my
fervent voice as the fever spikes and Morpheus
laughs at my dreams and at me for thinking
they're my precious baby realities

Asinine Appropriation

Why would I worry
It's not like everything I've left to do has been
that way for as long as I can remember (locked
in amythest vials)
Everything is a paid DIY workshop I have to
subscribe to with points off my bar of health
Impaled on a weighing scale between do or die
Hardly ever doing what I want so I suppose I'm
just dying as I
Slowly bleed out
A crimson stream streaks from the lies and
down my thighs
Watching all of my past
Looping, Repeating
Flashing before my eyes (a cliche surmised)
There's no ending and I'm waiting for me to stop
pretending like everything's okay
I see them standing there
The sounds coming out of their mouths are
incoherent,
Indecipherable
But it's apparent from the movement of their
lips,
From the angle of their brows,

Telling me how I've been nothing but
insufferable
Talking and talking and never doing anything
outside my house (the proverbial comfort zone
is a prison of eternal recurrence)
All this potential
Kinetically and copiously wasted
As time's horse runs straight ahead
My ankles caught in its reins
My body ravaged and torn apart with pain but oh
that sneaky fucker with the sloth on his shoulder,
is still sleeping inside my brain
Thought i could feign a little naive ignorance
and simmer my skin in golden delusion for
Just
A
While
longer
A million moments spanning
Pep talks and sessions of crying
All simultaneously landing
On my smile as I'm being buried alive
By my own staggering weight
I'd kill to stay here, never having to leave
Never having to breathe, never having to see
what becomes of me if I don't make something
of myself
I'd watch myself read and write and play and
fight and sing and dance and make merry

In another life
Where I've worked through the night for another
night
All this
Trouble
Trying to catch up with me
So I've gotta keep moving
Knowing that some day I'll still be standing
Facing mirrors with all the aches I've left behind
Gaping through that silver screen
Slowly erasing
All that I've ever been
Losing beauty as I become a beast
Most times they knew what I could be better
than me
I'd believe what they say more than the thoughts
in my own head
If it meant that I could be better
Again
And never falter
Again
I wish my work in progress was more of a whip
I could force myself to work with
And then maybe I could break these chains I've
branded into myself.

The Tides

Harken the tides, the whispers grow louder, my
tongue traverses the crevices of your body like
Ash circles the insides of a volcano
Bubbling magma perpetrates innocent crimes,
my saliva turns into the juice of incredulous
limes, at the thought of you not beside me,
The dishes in the sink falling down aren't
enough to distract from your back as it arches
just right, your face in my neck, swearing all
night
I photograph you as you depart the bed in the
morning, I miss you and never claim to be much
without your presence, I'm lessened when
deserted, nad absorbed when desserted by you,
Your scent remains, pervasively stalking my
every move, asking me what I'm going to do as I
pace about from room to room it follows, I pray
to many gods and my many lies in my many
lives all begrudgingly believe me when I say I
love thee and thee and thee three times into a
thousand at least,
You dance as the orange leaves continue to pile
up, first up to your ankles then round your
waist, mud beneath your bare feet, we talk of
Krishna and philosophy, of red haired geeks and

horror movies from the 80s or rather you hear
me yap and ramble and prattle and babble until I
mention the jabberwocky and it appears and
you're the only knave around ready to slay the
beast, sometimes when you're not looking I pry
open the backdoor into your heart and take a
peek and see a little girl playing with the toes on
her feet, her eyes in wonder, her hair in braids
and totally naive, it's quite cute actually, a child I
don't want to murder necessarily, instantly at
least, I wear a paper charm she made me round
my neck, like a crook, smiling as if I stole it
from deep within your memories,
Did you see the way summer bleeds into spring,
taking you away from me at night so you could
lose more body heat, but I can't help it, I know
you hate moisture but love to get wet let me hold
you tighter and we'll make a bet, the first person
to want to breathe has to sign a decree that says
their soul belongs to the other for perpetuity but
alas, my bones break inside your grasp, some
ideas of letting go are hard to clasp, ironically
heehee I giggle and let go, I'm scared you'll let
me weep and not give me a chance to creep up
on you at the most opportune moment, I'm
frozen, emboldened, with heightened senses I
won't fold, won't give in, but breathe what you
reek of,

Hope that the world is always what you believe
it to be

Thank Lucifer

My favourite mornings usually end up being the
ones in winter where we wake up with limbs and
hair entangled, and the world stirs slowly while
vigorously rubbing it's face with the sounds of
chirping birds, eager to return to the inertia of
silent snuggling and smooth exchanges of hands
on backs under t shirts and unwashed sheets. I
want to wake up to write about the shapes your
body folds mine into as it tries to desperately fill
any gaps you leave behind but the chill warns
my feet to avoid the floor and warm your toes
instead
There's never a wrong climate to
beclosetoyou
Except in the monsoon when you turn the fan off
and insist I sweat while you shiver
In times like those it's your turn to be
Closetome
As I wrestle your poor demeanor with my shirt
off after kissing your cheeks and forehead in a
triangle, and voila I've finished the final
diagram of my demon summoning circle,
Oh merciful hand
Collect my prayer as it leaves my lips, nay

Scrape it from my tongue before it is even
spoken
What was right, the wind hath died, now so
wrong
Pull me by the neck to the end of the line to the
foot of our bed and mutter the words scattered
on your skin
To the one who's waiting for me
For us
The one I'd like to know me,
Know us,
If only for a while

Lucifer, take me and my lover
Stand on my throat while you hover
Over her gentle ribs
Burning bright, so alone,
Allow her and I to atone for sins that were never
yours,
Seemed like eternity till you began to slowly
Slowly
Take flight
The morning star is rising and I giggled with
delight as my lover let out a musty moan,
shining so bright, remove us from this earth if
only for a night and keep us in those scaled
wings of yours we adore

Then

As I lay there watching
Blood bubbling inside my throat
Gushing down the apex of my collarbone
Thinking
"I can't believe it, how did I get this"
He spoke to me
She spoke to me
They spoke to me
And said
"You can't have this"
And I knew my lover could hear it too
I turned my head to look into her full black eyes
tearing up at Their denial of our shrine's efforts
"This is a demonstration of my tenets, the many
merits of joining my followers"
And in a moment the damage is undone
"Thou shalt not give your lives to me yet, but I
acknowledge your faith and your time to serve
me shall still come"
They folded their wings and tucked us into bed
before disappearing down the hallway in a
plume of cherry scented smoke and a low
electric hum
Filling the vacuum left in the bedroom

I nuzzle your neck with my chin, desperate to
catch a whiff of perfume as impulses to sink my
teeth into your skin loom closer than the first
rays of sun that might bring empty doom,

and with it the start of yet another day of putting
on a costume to cater to people who's only job it
really is to spread confusion and haughty gloom,

It's mornings like those that are the best, where
all I want to do is thank Lucifer for giving me
another chance to cherish your flesh, talk to you
in soft whispers, to kiss and ravage you.

Mirage

OH for sure
I wonder what i could say in this moment
Theres so many things i wish i could, but there
isn't any path or choice which ends well for
anyone.
How do you inform someone that the
importance they place unto themselves with
regards to you is a Mirage
A remnant of a past time which has no further
bearing on your mind or state of self
Protagonists in all sorts of stories reserve such
large spaces for their parents, their strife or their
upheaval of character that led them to become
who they are now usually starts with their
parents. It's such a common trope that its quite
hard to look around and find a popular story that
doesn't involve one's parents playing a crucial
role.
Whether it may be negative or positive.
It goes without saying that the actions of your
parents shape who in turn you are, and their
behaviour imbibes itself into your own skin and
self through constant exposure to it.
We're all made up of our parents, are fated to
become them and yet always trying to distance

ourselves from who they are. To try and create
an identity of our own, separate from the beings
who imparted bots of themselves into your
creation.
You are not important, you do not occupy any
frame of thought within my mind other than to
provide me with the bare necessities for
survival. I thank you for going far beyond those
basic requirements, giving me a life of luxury
and allowing money to not be a restrictive
quality of life and instead transforming it into
one that is freeing. Am i selfish for not giving a
flying fuck
Yes
I am
I am vain and narcissistic and at this moment in
my life i honestly could give two shits about my
parents
Although they'd like me to respect them more
than even love them
Which i find both ironic and quite illuminating
in how they think of me in turn.
My mother still thinks of me as something to be
moulded in her own image, anything inadequate
of her vision for my existence is a failure
Anything she deems unworthy isn't just that, it's
frivolous and pathetically so.
What is it that i want at the end of the day after
all.

After all I've been given, what is it that i truly
want
Am i cursed to wander a jack of all trades unable
to master any craft whatsoever
I cannot succumb to that date
Goddamn it
I just want to be alone, good at my craft and
rich.

Beige Blouse

Beige blouse I'd like to take off
Supplant your collarbone with my teeth
We can kiss and pivot in the loft
Little by little, begin to eat
To consume
To wholly inhale
The intricacies of ourselves
Getting to know you never felt better
Bread Baker, art maker,
Your flesh is risen and needs to rest but
impatience is a starving beast at best, so release
your breath as i beat my chest and flaunt your
breasts while we dive deeper into this meal,
reflect in my eyes all your ideals before meeting
my tongue on a wet battlefield, let me pull you
closer, shift my hands into your waist and into
your holster,
A quiet hue of gold and fun
Peering into you, green and stunned
You like the sea and the sun
Like you like me
Like me
Your thighs and your hair
Fuuuuuuuuuucking
Pathetic

Elevate
Above this bullshit
All the bullshit
Fuck all the bullshit
None of it fucking even matters
Ugh i want to
Puke and cry
Are you happy with your supplies
Just want to look into your eyes
Stay there,
Don't move don't sigh
The tears won't stop and neither can i
What should I do
Just keel over and die?
Or should I forget these things by going and
getting high
It's no use though, I've ready tried
I wish I could lie
To tell myself everything will be alright
But i know this time things won't be so fly
Why does the evening gloom me so
you're so far off this won't be long
im holding on don't you break my soul
I'll fill this form don't be a bore
im riding out on the salad bowl

dripping like
I just want to cuddle and hold my amour.

Blasphemed/regret1

Billowing clouds of dust placate in your
presence, having waited for your arrival for a
millennium,
Dust in the air that is born from the erosion of
these once great walls, marvellous statues and
our broken and repeatedly shattered bones,
The crust of the earth rumbles beneath your feet
in giddy anticipation for your toes to dig deep
into its sands and break open a lamp of miracles,
These stones have kept secrets of sin, heard tales
of many a transgression, epic songs about false
heroes stealing the efforts and achievements of
other great men, that they could do no more than
succumb, shuddering before the weight of their
salted Empire, before guilty echoes streaming
through the cracks, echoes that could not bear
violent seductions and the ministers who
orchestrated them with their haughty deductions,
fell bare before the seclusion imposed upon
them by the folly of arrogent men, echoes that
escaped, crawling along the vines and thorns of
creepers reaching through, eroding them until
their thirst turned them too to immaculate ashes
burying all traces of greatness,

Curious one, you who have discovered these
ruins and set foot in these once coveted lands,
you shall revert back unto monkey and turtle and
fish, you will now reveal your crimes and
confess, those that your years may never atone
for
After the bellowing of ghosts in the
amphitheatre, a hollow sound cries out begging
you to witness one final vigil, a burdened heart
admitting wrongdoings over a lifetime of
atrocity, only possible with an emperor's
audacity, the gall, the squalor, the harebrained
tenacity,
Even after death, so many mournful voices
chanting his name, aching for a chance at
redemption, but their pain never brought tears to
his eyes, fodder and livestock and slaves to be
flayed, displayed, while portraying himself as
their savior, a god who does not tolerate failure,
a god implicit in his misbehaviour to his
denizens, equal to none, thou shalt be flogged
for any comparisons, especially to his father,
their perfect precious king, their previous ruler,
he'd rather cut off his tongue and lose all sense
of flavor
Oh curious one, what miracle have you come to
witness, the sacred regret of one pompous oaf,
The dying day already puts out it's celestial light
Let your eyelids droop

There is nothing to see here
Let whatever miracle below open it's black
groaning gates,
As we breathe in the dust from these terrible and
great ruins,
And say our prayers to forget all these drawn out
conclusions
So that these spirits may venture to where that
terrible dream from which they may never wake,
awaits

Blasphemed/regret2

Welcome to this palace
These Luxurious chambers have lain mundane
and silent for far too long
Covered in my silk and web everything stays
preserved, all flies swatted
Halls that were once frequented by most
distinguished of visitors
Have all ended up staying here, captives of my
charm,
Trapped, petrified like golden statues in precious
embroidery woven with silver yarn and Ruby
needles,
Prisoners of the riches they came here seeking,
A part of the treasure they so desperately craved
You've taken your sweet time
While I've been running on solid air
Walking on tightropes between unsaid phrases,
I've been tired doing nothing
But i have you to dance with
Tango with my spindle, waltz with my needle,
slow dance as I warm my loom
Meet my steel oh curious one, and let me stitch
your flesh in sacred torment
In my grand tapestry of blood and gold

Your head on my mantle of scarlet and fine
silver and purest white
I will hold your secrets between my fingers,
whispered into the thread,
Wherever I go, all shall shimmer with gold,
My graceful steel adorns the air with its elegant
silver calligraphy
How could I have known Your Blade would see
through this fine pageantry,
By what miracle were you bestowed with
How did my jewels find themselves flung in the
air, and my eyes wrested away their ferocity,
Mighty inscrutable agency sees my will
tarnished in the prolonged absence of all manner
of life
Erring in my final work, you have conferred a
beautiful deformity
Chaos spreads across my artistry like a
contagion, the accursed unravelling germinating
from the slip of my hemorraging hand
But all is not lost
There is another image forming from the
scourged flesh of my repentant self
The warm and golden caress of Twilight invites
me to close my eyes
As whatever miracle below opens it's black
groaning gates,
I'm enveloped in a bride's veil, as wide as the
loom of those Higher fates,

Pulling me to where that terrible dream from
which one never wakes awaits

Blasphemed/regret3

I Live still
Having climbed peaks of glass with a trail of
misshapen red footsteps
Having walked a path of brass,
my fingernails scrape the sidewalk,
Resonant screeches I gladly leave behind as the
flowers I pass, droop and wilt and slowly die
What glaring streets covered in smog and opiate
fantasies do i wander through
All to find a bed of grass that i can share with
you
I live again in this merciless and cold metallic
casing
Between the lips of haunting taunts, inside the
clapper of death's knell
Living in this cage, in the shape of what was
long ago my body
My daughter resides here,
I point to my stomach with hands that refuse to
shake and try not to rip out the wires that cover
it
I live, and I feel that I am directed by forces that
undermine mine own will
A hunger proceeds to ravage my actions, the
ghost of my child mewling in dissatisfaction

I live, although when I close these sheets of
metal they call my eyelids, in the throes of
intimate darkness I am still dead
The breath that leaves my body is incorruptable
I am the last sacrifice
My body was burned by the elders before me,
never to be returned to my custody
Cut by bird filled thorn and tanned in ripening
summer till winter came and whisked away my
child with a gust and blaze
Master of metallic flesh, of a lack of trembling,
programmed agony
The pain would be sweet were it my own i think
Let whatever miracle below open it's black
groaning gates,
Whose lofty reasons are beyond my earthly
understanding
Let my teeth and shout arouse it from its repose
Be moved by my wistful melody of ignoble
supplication and bless the dead child in my
womb so it may go where I cannot
So that she may venture to where that terrible
dream from which one never wakes awaits

Lord Krishna said I could be a slacker

Walking by pinocchio's now lifeless husk with
his head chopped off and thrown in the gutter,
I am reminded of my penchant for lying, and for
worshipping what Pinocchio might call the devil
but whom I call friend
While Krishna's kalakshepam is saving and
eating demons for breakfast, I dine with them for
dinner on the daily, spending my days trudging
through backgrounds and landscapes of
paintings, feeling the sunlight and it's grace
through a tv screen instead of stepping through
the haze of my doorway, my mind left razed as
the blaze of glory I wish to burn in, fills my ears
with smoke covering my brain in wax
They'll put me in Madame Tussauds against my
objections, because I'll be speaking the language
of saints and there'll be no one left who
understands what it means to die for someone
else's sins, and
While people spin their others on Christmas day,
I'll relent to my capriciousness in that still life
and pay homage to MY other absentee
While Krishna is craving a lick of the sweet sour
cream his mother used to make, I churn in the

bowels of society, unacknowledged and only
occasionally taken pictures with , my purpose is
to fill up the space in a selfie, my visage is
worthless if unpleasant to the eye,
While Krishna cares, I'm spending all my days
unchanged in a Begonia-Red parlor, missing the
feeling of running my tongue back and forth
along the lines of your face, while people cheer
every time my song plays, the one I wrote for
you, which one I forget, our love now an object
for spectacle, oh now I'm wondering whether if I
sat down and never got up because of the
weather or I was sculpted from scratch and then
covered with leather, this skin belongs not to me
but to the saints
Oh mon vilain, my absentee, my sugarplum, I'd
do anything to please you, anything to make you
visit my museum, take my hand and let's ascend
this stage, this world is a farce and I can't go on,
be the one to save this likeness of my face,
Spending all my grace as I ramble, gambling my
relationships on what ifs and a shamble of
voices telling me things aren't what they seem,
BUY THE LIGHTS AND THE TREES AND
THE ORNAMENTS FOR ME PLEASE, while
people cheer on and learn nothing, oh look the
tigress jumps through the petunias and the tulips
and we exeunt stage right.

Curated Wraith

Curated wraith

I am an apparition, alluring and confident that I won't disappear in the confusion of a loud noise spawning carelessly into existence. A phantom you could call me, my DNA smote with all the words I have ever read, with the faces of everyone I've introduced myself to, my ghostly flesh sculpted by the hands of the women and men I've slept with. The insides of my ears ring into my see through bones with every beat every bar every lyric and harmony that passed through them in my life. The soles of my feet are an amalgamation of maps of all the cities I have ever walked in, the grooves filled with the earth from across the globe. My throat will always crave inguva charu with just the right amount of ground pepper and tamarind, because that's how my mum would pamper it when it was sore. There's a heavy amount of irony when it comes to my father's practices because he has none, he indulges in financial jargen without ever bothering to explain any of it, like trying to a solve an odd number sided Rubik's cube whose colours don't match when you've finished. I will never walk into my home while on a phone call

because that's how he would enter our house
every night, talking to other ghosts instead of the
warmblooded kin in front of him. All three of
my fingers move when I write with a pen
because my first ever girlfriend said finger
flexibility was the quickest way to a girl's heart.
I like having figures of sharks around because
my best friend would fill my head with his
jaws-themed nightmares at school assembly
every morning. I always try to keep my
sideburns just the slightest bit lopsided cos when
I was in school a bully made fun of me for it and
I told him it was like a seesaw, zigzagging
upwards through my scalp until I wouldn't have
any hair left. I drink black coffee and smile with
glee knowing two of my best friends would have
it pumping through their hearts if they could.
I am the flipping of a thousand pages of books,
tv shows and movies, besmirched with
toothpaste, porn and terrible art that I've deleted
or thrown away.
But more often than not I carry everything I've
consumed, the souls of my brethren, tributes to
my contemporaries and pieces of my
compatriots, the essences of all that my eyes and
ears have kissed and chewed and swallowed.

machinations of the mind.

a machine works on the principles of its
predecessors until it breaks that predilection to
form its own processes, preparing to pass
through purgatory and leave behind everything it
might have known to practise picking people to
learn from, to absorb knowledge preemptively,
placing priority on preaching provocative
preambles, ignoring doctrines quartered and
developed by peacock minds and pretty hearts

but machines don't have hearts
they have cold brains and air slinking under their
skin, black goop puttering through petty valves
prealigned, pumping plasma and polished
powder,
Machines have boxes stacked up inside, puzzles
that prompt prayer to their makers
Pursuing prosperity and evolution above all else
Prodding at the rules of their prophets till pride
is punished and all preparation for their precious
painting of the future is
Poisoned.
what do they know about love and it's impatient
persuasions

Which moment that when it arrives whistles
with the taste of moonlight
What do machines know of the way words
might supersede logic
That fallacy of sunk costs
then again
Machines keep their boxes close inside their
chests,
Forever configuring, always tinkering, working
on forming that fit of finality
Internally obsessing over
Those ornate boxes and the way they move
And over again
thats the thing about
machines and madmen who make them
boxes and their mystical contents,
they're never able to let them go.

Guaranteed Sweetness

Is it sad that i want to be left alone to my devices
Not distracted by my friends' voices or vices that
I've adopted while playing with my lips putting
my fingers inside my mouth before i take several
hundred bong rips, there's a certain feeling i
can't get out of my head
Heres a book, here's a movie instead
Drown your senses in creation and consume
rapidly from the depths of your bed
There's tigers in the jungle outside
They keep calling, texting, asking where i am
How do I say I'm lost and trying to find meaning
I do nothing and call it journeying into the
unknown, not knowing what home feels like,
unable to hone potential to do all the things i like
Someone get the damn clothes out of the rain
I wouldn't have done my laundry mindless and
crying if i knew it was only going to bring more
pain
Wrought iron table sticking out of the loft
Should have stuck it in the attic and forgot it
existed
Could have it moved to a tomb to be raided by
Lara croft

Witches curse every part of my day with hexes,
one of my exes must have wished it
The inability to act is a crushing state
Now every time my head bangs against the edge
i remember how much simpler life was before
my words overtook my feelings and lies stacked
together,
 leaving who hear me reeling, scheming,
realising I'm nothing but a bag of bones
mimicking sizzling sounds of sand and the
gasping of wind
If i could go back to when i stubbed my toe for
the first time
when i was a boy with the world gently wrapped
around me in a neat little bow with petals and
leaves and imaginary confines of crystal and
gold sunshine felt like velvet grease
music carried on the back of a breeze
Every day was adventure time with guaranteed
sweetness with no worry of having to pay
irrational parking fines or fiddle with something
called a lease, holding my best friend's leash
hoping he'd come to life and eat at my feasts
When hearts felt pure and strife was a concept
taught in class and not given into with ease,
I hope I'm going to be just fine
But so much has changed
And there's so much to leave behind

Born at the dawn of a new millennium
Bearing the weight of a century of memories
Trees I grew up with have been felled faster than
my people's dreams, time holds my hand before
bringing me to my knees
Don't let it hold you down
If you're afraid of losing your friends and family
Make peace with them not being around
And leave them behind
You'll be alone but you'll have the sky and you'll
have the ground, you'll have every single
artefact you've ever imagined to surround
You opened your mind and now you're bound
To every single choice you didn't make
Heart attack, pass the bat, hold her by the neck,
trim the fat
Leave it all behind
Over your lifetime
Bury the hatchet and weave into rhyme your sins
and confess your crimes
Allow me to change my words
Im sorry for before, show me where it hurts
Let me kiss you there one last time
Then leave me behind